PARSING IMAGINATION

poems by

Konstantin Prokos

Finishing Line Press
Georgetown, Kentucky

PARSING IMAGINATION

Copyright © 2016 by Konstantin Prokos
ISBN 978-1-944251-45-1 First Edition
All rights reserved under International and Pan-American Copyright Conventions.
No part of this book may be reproduced in any manner whatsoever without written permission from the publisher, except in the case of brief quotations embodied in critical articles and reviews.

ACKNOWLEDGMENTS

After Reading Henry James, *University College Quarterly,* Michigan State University, E. Lansing, Michigan, Spring 1974
In the Woodlot, Tom in the Garden, Canyon, *Northern Stars,* Powers, Michigan, March 2006
Pale Laughter, *Freefall,* Taylor, Michigan, August 2007
Walking in the Park, *Pegasus,* Boulder, Nevada, Fall 2010
Learning to Read, *Art on Ice,* Marquette, MI, March 2012

Editor: Christen Kincaid

Cover Art: Konstantin Prokos

Author Photo: Christine Lund-Prokos

Cover Design: Konstantin Prokos

Printed in the USA on acid-free paper.
Order online: www.finishinglinepress.com
also available on amazon.com

Author inquiries and mail orders:
Finishing Line Press
P. O. Box 1626
Georgetown, Kentucky 40324
U. S. A.

Table of Contents

At Sea 1

Pale Laughter 2

After Reading Henry James 3

Image 4

Cleriviews 5

Chicory 6

Too Poor 7

In the Woodlot 8

Hearing a String Quartet 9

School Morning 10

Still Life 11

October in the River 12

The Matriarch At 85 13

Learning to Read 15

In Oaxaca 16

Four Seasons 17

Tom, in the Garden 19

Distances 20

Tom, Redux 21

Stones on the Beach 22

Canyon 23

Walking in the Park 24

Keeping Time 25

In the Tropics 26

Thanks to my wife Christine, who gets me through various computer crises, and to Deno and Anastasia

AT SEA

The edge between Aegean sky
And cerulean sea
 Lies ambiguous:

Mountains or Naxos or Antiparos
Reconceive the edge
No longer a precipice.

Greeks saw it,
Emerging from the mist,
A place to sail for, like Santorini,

Where they could stand
On the rim of the caldera
And dream of sailing on.

PALE LAUGHTER

Three ladies in a summer tea scene
Taking instruction in ennui
Laugh like disconnected grackles.

What do they know of emptiness
The cruel mirth of human laughter
Sunbeams falling across an afternoon tea scene?

The grackle in the grass
Unaware of the equinox
Satisfies his appetite on old bagels.

Under the gazebo shade
The ladies, unprepared for rain
Shift on their buttocks

And shuffle their cards again.
These ruffled ladies among hearts and diamonds
Think summer's thunder false.

Their titter is like the startled bird's feather
Drifting though the heat.
He did not need to be told the rain would come

Yet he was surprised.
After the first drops of hot rain
The ladies unanimously throw down their cards

(As if each understands the quiver in her breast)
Ignore the grackle on parade
And shift on their buttocks again.

AFTER READING HENRY JAMES

It's hell
After a week
Of hacking through
With unslaked thirst
The tall rhetoric
The thick syntax
To wander into
The light of a clearing
And stumble on
A subtle blade of grass.

IMAGE

Pine wisp all awry
Wind bent through ages
Where mountain meets the sky

CLERIVIEWS
(After Edmund Clerihew Benton)

Ding dong
paradigm
ring around
a polemy
penny's worth
o' poesy
pocket full
o' heresy
patterns fall
on the wall
makes a man
hell see
how I pun
cture yer
sinsetivity
like a balloon
goes pop goes
wows the wine
for all goddamn
to drink
and stink
if think
they (of
coarse) Kant
Cheops chop
the corners
off a square
who didn't dare
by jeez
by jazz
cant
ilever
inta bed
a head
of Time
In Memoriam.

CHICORY

Heat dances upward
From the pavement in waves
Spreading across the road.
Across the road spreads
A shimmering blue mirage
Like the sea
Beckoning sailors and prodigals
Like me to venture
Toward the future
Along the bright silent highway.
Along the yellow center line
Comes a hum
Louder and louder.
Louder and louder
I thrust up my thumb
Until the hum fades
With quiet sweeping
Over the solitude and
The courage of the chicory
Lining the dry gravel shoulder
Bluer than the sky
Tall and strong
Where nothing else
Grows.

TOO POOR

Too poor
To buy a rose
When the gypsies played
In the old café on the avenue,
The balalaika and the tambourine
Became the act of love. I touched
Your gesture, saw your eyes, felt your voice
And scribbled a lifetime of unfinished poems
Because I didn't know how to talk the truth of love.

When you drifted into the snowy fields of memory
I learned when and how not to love
Made my way in the world
That was larger yet smaller
Brighter yet darker
Fuller yet emptier
And grown older
Saw the ways
Of love.

IN THE WOODLOT

Where they were
Stag and doe
Still in the still air,
An aged hound,
His hackles raised
With animal pleasure
Snuffles in the scented grasses
Of the woodlot,
Leaves his mark and
Scratches the earth.

Behind his dimmed eyes,
His nose to the wind,
He is running with the pack.

HEARING A STRING QUARTET

In the courtyard, these strings
And their music make memory
Of an ancient agon,
A dim and subtle fury.

"Music is feeling then not sound"—*
A memory stirred, a history of pain,
The Cedar Waxwing seized in flight,
A Mourning Dove or lonely swan.

A Red Tailed Hawk
Circumscribes the sky,
Drops like minor chords
A slow and fierce cry.

The hawk is a hunter
Feeding on furtive prey.
Memory too is furtive
But burrowed deep.

* Wallace Stevens, Peter Quince at the Clavier

SCHOOL MORNING

The ground hog hides in his burrow
The sparrows huddle in the bush
And the maples, leafless, have gone gray.

In the rain, the cold
Forms a thin ice on tree limbs,
Penetrates to the bone.

Traffic hisses down the road
Past children who hunch their way to school
And lights go out as the darkness lifts.

STILL LIFE

For Bob Caskey, Artist
In Memoriam

Soft October light drapes
Across the eggplant and the grapes
Poised like intuition
Next to an apple or a pear.
A syntax
Of light and hue painting
The fruit an almost palpable harmony,
Perhaps any
Still life is tentative.

When the shadow
Passes over the purple shapes
Framed in the window
And the reflection is right,
Like an air of cellos
The artist draws
The meditation of pears,
Sketches a pattern in the air.

OCTOBER IN THE RIVER

Through a sunny spot on the river
Between the box elder and sumac
A bass two hands long
Swims up stream.
Over it a flotilla of
Yellowed leaves
Sails down toward the dam
Heaping up in
Gathered wreckage of low water
Until sodden, they
Sink to the bottom.

THE MATRIARCH AT 85
(Kyriakoula Prokos 1908-2001)

This is now a brief and passing moment
Like the breeze and misty sea above Kyparissi,
The light of whitewash against the mountain stone,
Of olive, and dusty purple on the vineyard grape

The maiden's dowry, a sea journey to America,
Escape, sickness, adventure, terror, and discovery—
These are memories for all to own,
A guide to beginnings, endings, and renewal.

Look now at old sepia toned photographs
Corners cracked and unglued. Names bent
And forgotten fall between the album leaves.
Cloche hats and moustaches glower at the Brownie.

There's Uncle Leo, Christo, Gus, and Magdalena too
(Who sat for us while mama worked after the depression).
She grew house-like one after another.
What a depression we must have been.

Breaking toys and bones, hooking apples,
Firing a .22 slug though Old Lady Lizzie's window
Dark boy-men raging, bruising other lives.
You, loving first, understanding, praying, forgiving,

Made the sign of the cross and thought
Of the frescoes of saints in Aiyios Theodoros
Wedding chapel on the mountain,
Those morose eyes rubbed out by Turks.

When big Sammy Panayotikopoulos shook the barn
By the victory garden, we knew it had to come down.
Yet the same wood rose again for the '48 Plymouth,
In time, we all rose, our beards gone from black to gray.

Memory is long, Love is long,
From village to town
From stony mountain to reedy beach
From birth to grave to birth again.

Now, when you tell the truths of time's unfolding,
Our recognition of your endurance opens—
Our recognition opens like poppies
On a sunny hillside under Peloponnesian sky.

LEARNING TO READ

As a child
Dreaming in the dark cupboard
Under the stairs

Imagining, among
Old country linens
Christmas wreaths of worn velour
An old brass bugle
Mothballs in an old trunk
And secret boxes

I learned the art
Of reading my senses
And became a prodigal
On the endless road home,

A journeyman of touch
A mariner on a sea of smell
A voyager of seeing
In a shimmering darkness.

IN OAXACA

Lacy Jacaranda in her royal dress
Gives no courtyard shade
Her beauty races across the skin
Tastes of lemon ices
And makes a shudder in the moment

Zapotecos in the market place
Cool beneath the horned Pochote
A spiky bark too fierce for child play
Its green parasol moves above the amaryllis
Like a tango or a samba.

No utile tool these trees
No hammer, saw, or nail
No needle, thread, or cloth
No house, or suit of clothes,
Or shield in time of war.

Jacaranda and Pochote
Stir the mind,
Write a history for the senses,
Nothing less,
Nothing more.

FOUR SEASONS

Winter

I
Cardinal call
Gentle breeze
Hemlock, balsam tall
And calm at ease
In silent snowfall

II
Crow calls
Three trees
Barren, tall
Snow flurries casting gray, a pall

Spring

I
Finches going
Gray to gold
On branches budding
Soon to blossom
Into sweet surprise

II
Long necked Robin, pretty
Pulling worms
Is a carnivore that eats berries
In desperation

Summer

I
Mourning Doves
Paroo Paroo
Keeping cool
Under the cedar boughs
'til roosting time

II
Circling high
On the thermals
Naked headed buzzards
Search for carrion in the dry fields

Autumn

I
Red leaves falling
Sand Hill Cranes leaving
Stubble in the bare fields
The moon is crisp,
The air is cool

II
Geese quarrel in the bay—
Fly away or stay—
Huddled on the morning ice
Waiting for the sun.

TOM, IN THE GARDEN

Ordinary Tom lurks in the garden glade
And grackles curse in the bracken
By the gazebo shade.

Tom's restraint
Is like the feint
Of lovers in the garden
Whose smile and whisper

Glance and stiffen
In the lilac air
As if only they could care
How love becomes a burden.

Sometimes, looking at
The face of a cat,
You will see no expression there,
Only a whisker twitching in the air.

DISTANCES

A child dreaming, lying
In the open fields at night,
With a slight turn
Can see from Polaris to the Pleiades

Sun and moon east and west
Shine in the semi-darkness
As the dew gathers
At morning

Wordless the young couple
In the steamy car
Compress the distance with heat
To work their dreams

The lamplight by the wing chair
Falls on the open book of Browning
The reader is far away

In the parlor
He and she by the fire
Warm themselves in the cold air
Tense neither speaks

In an embrace
The distance between the lips
And the kiss
Is anticipation that lasts forever

You walk forward
You walk along side
You walk ahead

TOM, REDUX

In the garden, you have the cat posing
Nearby, you have Finches objecting
Over by the honeysuckle
The Calico, crouched,
Unsettles them, him and her
Holding hands and watching,
Laughing at the cat,
Worrying about the song birds.
The lovers drop hands.
Unsure,
She twirls an aster,
He snaps off a zinnia
And wordless they
Return to the house.

STONES ON THE BEACH

The stones on the beach
Do not weep.
The simpering is only the surf
Pushing in and out against

The shore. The pines in the dark wood
Stooped like suppliants
Do not sigh with grief—the whisper
Is merely the wind passing through.

And now the rain comes
After the long dry spell.
It is not carried by prayer or
Dances to the gods.

Strange weather around the world,
Rising or falling through the poisoned air,
Brings too much rain here or not enough there
And calamity everywhere.

CANYON

At three every afternoon
The sky darkens and the wind shifts,
Slinks across the canyon,
Tenses with a few drops of rain.

The People have been leathered
By sun and wind.
In season, the cholla blooms
And Spirits rise in the mountains.

WALKING IN THE PARK

In Madrid
In the park of the Crystal Palace
Among the box and yellow roses in bloom
I met the dead poet Calderon.

        He said

Eat with the lust of lovers
Love with the enthusiasm of the glutton
Deaden your senses with excess

              And put an end to desire.

KEEPING TIME

          Sit still
And listen. Is the tick
And tock
Just a trick
Of the clock?

          Be still.
Make the tick
With an act of will
Become a rock
On which to stick

          A bill
To make a change
In keeping time
From tick tock tick tock
To tock tick tock tick.

          If you will
You might be shocked
To find you cannot interdict
The rhythms of the clock
Unless you smash it with a brick.

IN THE TROPICS

Day after day in the dry season
Rain falls on the flooded Sarapiqui.

At dawn, a howler monkey, high in the Mangrove trees,
Sends his summons over the canopy.

Toucans and Oropendula huddle
In the plantain and palm.

All day, Ticos, out of sorts,
Wait for the front to pass:

This change in the weather, a puzzle
Testing the memories of old men.

Konstantin **Prokos** was born in Escanaba, Michigan in 1937, the fifth son of Greek immigrants. He attended five different schools while working as a cook, cub reporter, DJ, TV announcer, and social worker before getting his BA from Oakland University, Michigan. He taught writing and speech/drama at Hazard Community College, Kentucky 1969 to1972 and writing and literature at CS Mott Community college in Flint, Michigan from 1972 to 1995.

In undergraduate school in Prokos was heavily involved in theatre while majoring in both theatre and English. Early on he was influenced by the work of Wallace Stevens; ultimately he found his own voice in the experience of growing up in Michigan's forests and waters of the Upper Peninsula.

Although he had been writing since his teens, Prokos published his first poem, written as a graduate student, in 1974. There followed a long hiatus while he raised his children and taught. Prokos says he only writes when ideas have "cooked" enough. He sometimes spends years changing or polishing a poem, reducing it "to say as much as possible in as few words as possible", a fundamental principle of poetry.

In 2010 Prokos published *A Word in Edgewise: Brief Essays on Language* based on scripts for a one-minute public radio program he created about word origins and usage. For the last 20 years, Prokos has also maintained a painting studio and has shown his work throughout the Midwest. Prokos continues to paint, write and publish.

www.ingramcontent.com/pod-product-compliance
Lightning Source LLC
Chambersburg PA
CBHW060226050426
42446CB00013B/3191